Especially for

_____

From

_____

Date

_____

Inspiring Thoughts
from the
Great
Outdoors

BARBOUR
PUBLISHING

ISBN 978-1-61626-164-1

Devotional selections are taken from *The Great Adventure Men's Devotional Journal,* published by Barbour Publishing, Inc. Writers include Tom Blubaugh, Stephen Fierbaugh, Steve Husting, John Long, Steve Mathisen, David McLaughlan, Paul Muckley, and Tracy Sumner.

All scripture quotations are taken from the HOLY BIBLE, NEW INTERNATIONAL VERSION®. NIV®. Copyright © 1973, 1978, 1984 by International Bible Society. Used by permission of Zondervan. All rights reserved.

Published by Barbour Publishing, Inc., P.O. Box 719, Uhrichsville, Ohio 44683, www.barbourbooks.com

Our mission is to publish and distribute inspirational products offering exceptional value and biblical encouragement to the masses.

 Member of the
Evangelical Christian
Publishers Association

Printed in China.

Contents

A Big, Beautiful World to Enjoy

If you love the outdoors, you're in good company.

How would you ever count the people worldwide who take part in hunting, fishing, or camping? Then there are the boaters, bikers, and hikers doing their thing in the sunshine and fresh air. And don't forget the rock climbers, the cave explorers, and those folks who just like to gaze up at the stars on a clear, dark night.

Yes, we love the outdoors. But why?

Maybe it's a kind of primal connection to God's creation. When the Lord spoke the universe into existence, He made our earth a perfect place for life—then formed humans from its very dust. We're actually a part of the world we live in! And though humans have failed in many ways—our earth is no longer Eden—we still inhabit a big, beautiful world that God kindly allows us to enjoy.

That's what *Inspiring Thoughts from the Great Outdoors* is all about—taking full advantage of this fun and fascinating planet of ours while drawing some life-enhancing lessons from it. Wherever your passions lie, you'll find something here to intrigue, challenge, or encourage you.

God speaks in many ways—and one of those ways is through His creation.

On the mountainside, in the woods, under the clear blue sky, wherever. . .let's be ready to listen.

Pitch a Tent

So Joseph also went up from the town of Nazareth in Galilee to Judea, to Bethlehem the town of David, because he belonged to the house and line of David. He went there to register with Mary, who was pledged to be married to him and was expecting a child. While they were there, the time came for the baby to be born, and she gave birth to her firstborn, a son. She wrapped him in cloths and placed him in a manger, because there was no room for them in the inn.

LUKE 2:4–7

Roughing It

When it comes to campers, the "roughing it" scale varies dramatically.

Some insist on an intimate connection with nature, eschewing even a tent. A sleeping bag under the stars is quite enough for them.

Others prefer a tent covering, but still lay on the ground. An air mattress seems right to some, while others like their tent to "pop up" from a trailer with pull-out beds. RVers camp in what are essentially rolling hotel rooms, featuring televisions, refrigerators, and showers.

Mary, soon to deliver the baby Jesus, could only dream of such a comfortable place to stay. With the Bethlehem inn declaring No Vacancy, Mary and her husband, Joseph, ended up in a cave or stable—nobody knows for sure, just that there was an animal feeding trough handy. There, in the most humble circumstances, the Creator and King of the entire universe was born as a helpless infant.

You could say Jesus was "roughing it" on earth—dramatically so some thirty years later when He died on the cross for our sins.

And aren't you glad?

*Who could have dreamed
that this little baby
would change the course
of the world?*

MARTIN BELL
The Way of the Wolf

Father God, this world can be beautiful—but it's nothing compared to the unimaginable glories of heaven. You sent Your Son here to make the way to heaven for everyone who will call on His name. Thank You for Jesus' willingness to "rough it" on our behalf. We'd be hopeless without Him!

This is the message we have heard from him and declare to you: God is light; in him there is no darkness at all. If we claim to have fellowship with him yet walk in the darkness, we lie and do not live by the truth. But if we walk in the light, as he is in the light, we have fellowship with one another, and the blood of Jesus, his Son, purifies us from all sin.

1 John 1:5–7

In the Light

Campers can't get enough of their favorite activity. No matter how many times we've been "out there," it never gets old. There are so many things to experience and enjoy:

- Cooking freshly caught fish on an open fire—scrumptious.
- Breathing fresh, open air—exhilarating.
- Sitting around a campfire with family and friends—uplifting.
- Lying in a sleeping bag under the moon and stars—awesome.
- Listening to the symphony of nocturnal creatures—tranquil.

But getting up in the wee hours, finding the flashlight dead, tripping over rocks, stubbing a toe on a tree root or turning an ankle in a hole—that's no fun at all.

That's exactly what life is like when we're separated from the true Light, Jesus Christ. Walk in the Light!

Whatever clouds you face today,
ask Jesus, the light of the world,
to help you look behind the cloud
to see His glory and His plans for you.

BILLY GRAHAM
Hope for Each Day

Lord, this world is so dark spiritually. There are so many dangers that can cause me to trip and stumble. But in Your light, Jesus, I can walk in safety and confidence. Please help me to see Your plans and ways, and to stay on the path You've set before me.

Now we know that if the earthly tent
we live in is destroyed, we have a building
from God, an eternal house in heaven,
not built by human hands.

2 Corinthians 5:1

Gone Fishin'

Whom have I in heaven but you? And earth has
nothing I desire besides you. My flesh and my
heart may fail, but God is the strength of my
heart and my portion forever. . . . As for me, it is
good to be near God. I have made the Sovereign
LORD my refuge; I will tell of all your deeds.

PSALM 73:25–26, 28

Celebrating God's Goodness

In the movie *A River Runs Through It*, a Presbyterian preacher and his two sons enjoy a day of fly-fishing in which all three men catch trout from Montana's Big Blackfoot River.

"I'd say the Lord has blessed us all today," the preacher says, looking at his sons' catches. Then he pulls a trout from his creel that dwarfs the boys' fish. With a smile, he says, "It's just that He's been particularly good to me!"

There's a great blessing in acknowledging that all good things—even something as simple as a successful day of fishing—come from the hand of our very good God. It's wonderful to know that He desires to do good for those who love Him.

When we tell others of God's goodness, we set ourselves—and them—up to receive further blessings from the hand of God. His love and generosity to those who love Him know no bounds.

All of my need He freely supplieth,
Day after day His goodness I prove;
Mercies unfailing, new every morning,
Tell me of God's unchangeable love.

THOMAS O. CHISHOLM
"He Supplieth All of My Need"

Remind me daily, Father, that You are the source of all good things—because You Yourself are good. Everything I have comes from You, and is for both my enjoyment and sharing with others. My needs, my wants— You freely supply, Lord, telling me every morning of Your unchangeable love. I celebrate that love!

Help, LORD, for the godly are no more; the faithful have vanished from among men. Everyone lies to his neighbor; their flattering lips speak with deception. May the LORD cut off all flattering lips and every boastful tongue.

PSALM 12:1–3

Boast in the Lord

Some fishermen are notorious for bragging. Who hasn't heard a particularly boastful angler talking with pride of his own prowess, as he caught the most fish and the biggest one of the day?

The humble angler, on the other hand—and the one most of us enjoy fishing with—is a man who loves seeing others in his party enjoy the same success he does. . .and who realizes that everything, even a successful day of fishing, is a gift from God above. He can use anything to illustrate biblical truth—including a day of fishing with your best buddy.

Remember that there's no better day of fishing than the one in which everyone comes out of it grateful to God for successes enjoyed. And remember to follow the apostle Paul's instructions: "Let him who boasts boast in the Lord" (2 Corinthians 10:17).

*If our hearts are full
of our own wretched "I ams"
we will have no ears to hear
His glorious, soul-satisfying "I am."*

HANNAH WHITALL SMITH
God of All Comfort

Father, may I never forget that any success
I enjoy is Your gift to me. Whether I've caught
the biggest fish, or received a promotion at work,
or raised the brightest kid, help me to remember
that You are the origin of all good things in my life.
May I boast only in You.

"Come, follow me," Jesus said,
"and I will make you fishers of men."

MATTHEW 4:19

Take a Hike!

Then God said, "Let us make man in our image, in our likeness, and let them rule over the fish of the sea and the birds of the air, over the livestock, over all the earth, and over all the creatures that move along the ground." So God created man in his own image, in the image of God he created him; male and female he created them. God blessed them and said to them, "Be fruitful and increase in number; fill the earth and subdue it."

Genesis 1:26–28

Outdoor Equipment

Technology keeps improving our outdoor equipment, from the mountain bikes and four-wheelers we ride to the GPS systems that tell us how to get back home.

But our most amazing equipment has always been right with us: the human body, handcrafted by God. Think of everything the body does on a "simple" hike: The legs propel the body forward, adjusting effortlessly to changes in terrain. Arms and hands provide balance and aid progress on particularly challenging trails. Eyes and ears take in the stimuli of the woods—the colors of the leaves, the sounds of the birds—and the brain analyzes that data without slowing the ongoing physical processes in the slightest.

Meanwhile, our conscious thoughts run from family to work to church to that funny movie we just saw. . .and maybe, if we're lucky, that gallon of milk we need to pick up on the way home.

There will never be a machine to compare with the human body!

He was made of the dust of the ground,
a very unlikely thing to make man of;
but the same infinite power that
made the world of nothing
made man, its masterpiece,
of next to nothing.

MATTHEW HENRY
Commentary on the Whole Bible

Thank You, Lord, for my amazing body, the very house of Your Spirit. May I honor You in the way I care for myself, whether I'm out on the trail or considering another (and unnecessary) helping at the dinner table. You created me to honor You, Lord— may I fulfill that duty physically as well as spiritually.

The path of the righteous is like the first gleam of dawn, shining ever brighter till the full light of day. But the way of the wicked is like deep darkness; they do not know what makes them stumble. . . . Make level paths for your feet and take only ways that are firm. Do not swerve to the right or the left; keep your foot from evil.

PROVERBS 4:18–19, 26–27

In the Full Light of Day

A couple was hiking and camping in a wilderness area. Rising early one morning, they packed their camp by lantern and hiked a length of trail by flashlight to a scenic overlook. Upon arriving, they dropped their packs and sat on a large rock, huddling together for warmth.

As the morning sun began to peek over the mountains, it slowly painted the valley below in blues and greens and the sky above in breathtaking reds and purples. But only when the sun was fully up and shining brightly could they see, far below them, the riverside trail they'd be taking that day.

That's a good picture of our lives. We spend a lot of time living and working in the dark—or by the limited light of our own wisdom. It's only when we let the light of God's Word shine on our lives that we can see where our true path lies.

Help me to walk
by the other light supreme,
Which shows thy facts
behind man's vaguely hinting dream.

GEORGE MACDONALD
Diary of an Old Soul

Creator God, help me to see the path You have set
for me by the light of Your Word. This world offers
so many roads, all of them leading to dangerous—if
not disastrous—places. But Your way—the narrow

you...

This is the way, walk...

Isaiah 30:21

Open Season

When Isaac was old and his eyes were so weak that he could no longer see, he called for Esau his older son and said to him, "My son." "Here I am," he answered. Isaac said, "I am now an old man and don't know the day of my death. Now then, get your weapons—your quiver and bow— and go out to the open country to hunt some wild game for me. Prepare me the kind of tasty food I like and bring it to me to eat."

Grateful for God's Provision

In Old Testament times, hunting wasn't so much a means of rest and relaxation as it is today. Men hunted because they needed food for themselves and their families. They knew that a failed hunting trip could mean going hungry—and for that reason they probably thanked God for success.

In our culture, though, hunting is generally done for recreation. Most outdoorsmen don't hunt because they have to; they do it because they enjoy it.

Whether a man hunts for need of food, like in the old days, or simply because he enjoys it, there is a common aspect: God is the One who blesses each endeavor and gives success.

Whether it's hunting or fishing, whitewater rafting or hiking that you enjoy, remember always to thank God. He wonderfully meets all your needs, and gives you a place to spend some of your "downtime."

Thy best Friend
is the Lord of Providence.
Thy Brother is Prime Minister
of the universe,
and holds the keys
of the divine commissariat.

F. B. MEYER
The Way into the Holiest

My gracious, generous Provider, I thank You for giving me everything I need—and more—to enjoy the life You've given me. Whether I'm hunting my food or buying it at the grocery store, I have plenty of healthy, good-tasting things to eat. I have my "daily bread" and much, much more. Thank You for taking such good care of me, Lord.

Do not be foolish, but understand what the Lord's will is. Do not get drunk on wine, which leads to debauchery. Instead, be filled with the Spirit. . . . Sing and make music in your heart to the Lord, always giving thanks to God the Father for everything, in the name of our Lord Jesus Christ.

EPHESIANS 5:17–20

Thanksgiving Dinner

There's little adventure in Thanksgiving dinner these days. The turkey, potatoes, stuffing, and pumpkin pie usually come from a nearby restaurant or grocery store.

But in 1621, generally acknowledged as the first such celebration in North America, Thanksgiving dinner required the men to go out hunting. "Our Governor sent four men on fowling," one colonist wrote. "They four in one day killed as much fowl as, with a little help beside, served the Company almost a week." Meanwhile, the Wampanoag Indians who joined the pilgrims "went out and killed five Deer."

And what was the big deal? In the words of the already-mentioned colonist, "that so we might after a more special manner rejoice together" over the good harvest God had provided.

Nearly four hundred years later, we do well to remember God's blessing, too. Starting today, let's make thanksgiving a staple of our diet.

He requires no great matters of us;
a little remembrance of Him from
time to time, a little adoration:
sometimes to pray for His grace,
sometimes to offer Him your sufferings,
and sometimes to return Him thanks
for the favours He has given you.

BROTHER LAWRENCE
The Practice of the Presence of God

Father God, I thank You for all that You've given
me—both physical and spiritual. May I always
remember to give You praise, "a little remembrance,
a little adoration" as Brother Lawrence put it.
Everything I have is a gift, a gift from Your gracious
heart. May I never forget Your blessings, Father!

The lazy man does not roast his game,
but the diligent man prizes his possessions.

PROVERBS 12:27

Journey to the Center of the Earth

Since we have a great high priest who has gone through the heavens, Jesus the Son of God, let us hold firmly to the faith we profess. For we do not have a high priest who is unable to sympathize with our weaknesses, but we have one who has been tempted in every way, just as we are—yet was without sin. Let us then approach the throne of grace with confidence, so that we may receive mercy and find grace to help us in our time of need.

HEBREWS 4:14–16

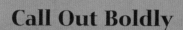

Call Out Boldly

The exploration of caves is called *spelunking*. Some have defined the term *spelunk* as "the sound of a forehead hitting a stalactite after running in terror in pitch blackness."

Wandering about in cold, damp darkness isn't everyone's idea of fun, but it can be instructive for all of us. For example, if you've made a bad turn in a cave and can't find your way back, disregard the impulse to move and simply stay put. Shout every couple of minutes to help your partner or a rescue party locate you. (And probably carry you out to treat that ugly bruise on your forehead.)

It's not only in the blackness of a cave that we lose our bearings. Life can be dark, confusing, and frightening at times, but God's advice is like that of the spelunking corps: Resist the impulse to run. Instead, simply rest where you are and call out to Him. God's ears are always open, and He's always ready to rescue.

Some people think
God does not like to be troubled
with our constant coming and asking.
The only way to trouble God
is not to come at all.

D. L. MOODY
Prevailing Prayer: What Hinders It?

Lord, may I draw near to You today, calling out boldly for Your help. Sometimes this life makes me feel like I'm in a cave—it's so dark I can't find my way, and that's never a good feeling. But with Jesus as my sympathetic helper, just waiting for my cry for help, I can't go wrong. Help me now, Lord!

Since my youth, O God, you have taught me,
and to this day I declare your marvelous deeds.
Even when I am old and gray, do not forsake
me, O God, till I declare your power to the next
generation, your might to all who are to come. Your
righteousness reaches to the skies, O God, you
who have done great things. Who, O God, is like
you? Though you have made me see troubles, many
and bitter, you will restore my life again; from the
depths of the earth you will again bring me up.

PSALM 71:17–20

From the Depths of the Earth

Mammoth Cave, in Kentucky, is the world's largest cave system. It has over 360 miles of tunnels and is still not fully explored and mapped.

As we walk, crawl, and wiggle through a maze of twisting little passages, all seemingly alike, it is easy to become claustrophobic. When all lights are extinguished, we experience true darkness like we've never "seen" before. Hands waved in front of faces are indistinguishable. Fears can quickly bubble up to the surface, and, left unchecked, can become panic.

Life can often be like Mammoth Cave. Are we in a fix? We probably descended by our own free will. But now, how are we going to get out? We definitely need the Light.

God sometimes allows us to get into trouble. But He will never be far from us.

As far as the Lord is concerned,
the time to stand is in the darkest moment.
It is when everything seems hopeless,
when there appears no way out,
when God alone can deliver.

DAVID WILKERSON
"Right Song, Wrong Side"

*Lord God, I've experienced much trouble of my own
making in this life—and sometimes it seems hopeless.
But the underlying message of Your Word is hope,
Father. Please bring me up out of these depths.
Show me Your great mercy and power to deliver.*

They went about in sheepskins and goatskins,
destitute, persecuted and mistreated—
the world was not worthy of them.
They wandered in deserts and mountains,
and in caves and holes in the ground.

HEBREWS 11:37–38

Two-Wheelin' It

Not that I have already obtained all this, or have already been made perfect, but I press on to take hold of that for which Christ Jesus took hold of me. Brothers, I do not consider myself yet to have taken hold of it. But one thing I do: Forgetting what is behind and straining toward what is ahead, I press on toward the goal to win the prize for which God has called me heavenward in Christ Jesus.

PHILIPPIANS 3:12–14

The Century

Ambitious bicyclists pursue "the century," a single-day ride of a hundred miles.

Aspirants prepare with a weeks-long training program. On the big day, they pack high-energy foods like grains, nuts, and fruits, along with plenty of water for proper hydration. Anticipation soaring, they pedal off to bicycling glory.

But for many, there's a "bonk," also known as "hitting the wall." Maybe they started too fast, forgot to eat or drink soon enough, or just weren't in as good of shape as they thought they were. Somewhere along the line, the century gets tough.

That's a lot like life. No matter how strong we think we are, there's often a bonk. It might be a physical problem, a troubled relationship, a nagging temptation. . . but it's real, and it's hard.

The apostle Paul's advice? Don't stop. Keep moving—straining even—toward Jesus, the goal of your heavenly century. You can do it!

Do not pray for easy lives,
pray to be stronger men.
Do not pray for tasks equal to your powers,
pray for powers equal to your tasks.

PHILLIPS BROOKS
"Going Up to Jerusalem"

Lord, when the journey gets hard, help me to stay the course, eyes always on You. Physical weariness is tough enough—if I'm out on a bicycle, taking a long hike, or just trying to keep up with my kids. But when I get tired spiritually, I absolutely need Your strength. Please keep me straining toward Jesus.

Do not be deceived: God cannot be mocked.
A man reaps what he sows. The one who sows to
please his sinful nature, from that nature will reap
destruction; the one who sows to please the Spirit,
from the Spirit will reap eternal life. Let us not
become weary in doing good, for at the proper
time we will reap a harvest if we do not give up.

GALATIANS 6:7–9

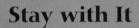

Stay with It

Hikers, bikers, and swimmers do well to remember this commonsense idea: Going out is always easier than coming back.

While you might feel fine on the first leg of the journey, the doubling back may leave you weary, blistered, and cramped—possibly even in danger. But if you travel too far on the way out, you can't just quit—especially if you're swimming. Somehow, you've got to find the reserves to keep moving toward home, like the hummingbird that flies, nonstop, over the Gulf of Mexico on its annual migration.

There's a parallel here to the Christian life. The apostle Paul encouraged us to "not be weary in well doing," to keep moving forward whatever the difficulties. We might be tired when we're done, but there is a reward— the reaping we enjoy "at the proper time."

We must not lie loitering in the ditch,
and wait till Omnipotence
pull us from thence.
No, no: we must bestir ourselves,
and actuate those powers
which we have already received.

HENRY SCOUGAL
Life of God in the Soul of Man

*Lord, I get tired on this journey. But, like the
hummingbird over the ocean, I'm too committed to
quit! Help me to "not be weary in well doing" and
never faint along the way. For my own good, and for
the well-being of those I love, empower me to move
forward in this Christian life. May I never quit
until I've reaped Your eternal reward.*

Wherever the spirit would go,
they would go, and the wheels would rise
along with them, because the spirit of the
living creatures was in the wheels.

EZEKIEL 1:20

Row, Row, Row
Your Boat

The LORD said to me, "See, I have begun to deliver Sihon and his country over to you. Now begin to conquer and possess his land." When Sihon and all his army came out to meet us in battle at Jahaz, the LORD our God delivered him over to us and we struck him down, together with his sons and his whole army. At that time we took all his towns and completely destroyed them.

DEUTERONOMY 2:31–33

Remember Past Victories

Imagine a family taking up kayaking on the river rapids—they don't tackle the most dangerous waters first. (Though Mom might tackle Dad, who came up with the whole crazy idea.)

Wise kayakers consider the "class" of a river before entering the water. Class I waters are easily navigated, while Class VI rapids are considered "unrunnable." Trained guides help less-experienced boaters advance through the levels.

In the spiritual life, God also trains in stages. He often allows us to experience small trials to give us confidence in His faithfulness. As we remember how He's helped us through, we build up hope and trust for the next, potentially larger, trial.

To strengthen the Israelites for coming warfare, Moses reminded them of battles they'd won with the Lord's help. Today, as we're faced with spiritual challenges, let's remind ourselves of past victories, too—always recalling the God who guided us through.

*When you finally meet the
One who made you,
and examine the lifelines
he has sent along the way,
you will at last understand
how every detail
made sense in the swirling reality
of life's blessings and threats.*

RAVI ZACHARIAS
The Grand Weaver

Lord, You have been my strength in the past. Now give me strength to overcome the new challenges I face. Whether I'm running the rapids of a fast-flowing river or navigating the shoals of my workplace, I need Your help to get through safely. You've helped me before, Father—please do so again!

Then he said to them all: "If anyone would come after me, he must deny himself and take up his cross daily and follow me. For whoever wants to save his life will lose it, but whoever loses his life for me will save it. What good is it for a man to gain the whole world, and yet lose or forfeit his very self?"

LUKE 9:23–25

When the Kayak Rolls

When we've rolled a kayak—it's upside down in the rapids with our head hitting rocks and our lungs bursting—everything in our flesh wants to claw our way upwards toward the surface. But this is precisely the *wrong* move.

To escape, we bend against the body's impulses, lean forward, and pull the release handle on the kayak skirt. Just a little tug pops the seal, allowing water to rush in and air to bubble out, carrying our body upwards with it.

Life is sometimes like the rocky rapids, as we're carried away, upside down, in the rush. Denying our fleshly nature and cravings is the most unnatural thing in the world. Indeed, the world says it is foolishness. But that's what Jesus commands of us. It's the only way to life.

*Your main concern lies
in dwelling continually
upon the God who is within you.
Then, without particularly
thinking of self-denial
or "putting away the
deeds of the flesh,"
God will cause you to experience
a natural subduing of the flesh!*

JEANNE GUYON
Experiencing the Depths of Jesus Christ

O Lord, You allow the rapids of life! Please bring
me through my own personal rapids, showing me
how to follow You by denying myself and taking up
Your cross. Sometimes Your way seems crazy—
but I know from experience and Your Word that
it's the only way to life. Protect me, Father.

Then Peter got down out of the boat, walked on the water and came toward Jesus. But when he saw the wind, he was afraid and, beginning to sink, cried out, "Lord, save me!"

MATTHEW 14:29–30

Climb Every Mountain

I have seen something else under the sun:
The race is not to the swift or the battle to
the strong, nor does food come to the wise or
wealth to the brilliant or favor to the learned;
but time and chance happen to them all.

Pole, Pole

Mount Kilimanjaro rises 19,340 feet above the African plain. Many flock to the challenge of climbing Africa's highest peak.

"Kili" may be climbed without technical skills, but the guides constantly remind the climbers, "Pole, pole. . ." It means "slow, slow" in Swahili. The guides know that those who start the day hiking fast and passing others will later be found by the side of the trail gasping for breath in the thin air. Those who succeed in reaching the summit of the world's highest free-standing mountain are those who have learned the secret of just putting one foot in front of the other, thousands and thousands of times in succession.

Our daily life is much like Kilimanjaro. God doesn't need us to be bottle rockets, making a loud pop but quickly fading away. Instead, He wants long-term faithfulness and growth. Truly rising in Christian maturity requires us to be steady and constant, weathering life's peaks and valleys.

Growth in godly character
is not only progressive and always unfinished,
it is absolutely necessary for spiritual survival.
If we are not growing in godly character,
we are regressing; in the spiritual life
we never stand still.

JERRY BRIDGES
The Practice of Godliness

God of the mountains and valleys, help me to remember every day that "slow and steady" wins the race. My spiritual journey is a marathon, not a sprint—and I'll wear myself out in the thin air of this world if I don't take time to refresh myself in You.

You are enthroned as the Holy One; you are the praise of Israel. In you our fathers put their trust; they trusted and you delivered them. They cried to you and were saved; in you they trusted and were not disappointed.

PSALM 22:3–5

In a Tight Spot

You're on a smooth rock face, hundreds of feet up. You need a handhold if you're going to go any farther, but there just isn't one to be found. There is a crack in the rock, but very little to grip. What to do?

Here's where you call on a friend. That's the affectionate name for a piece of climbing equipment also known as a spring-loaded camming device. Slip it into a tight space and it expands, gripping the rock. Then you can attach a carabiner, slip your safety rope through it, and relax. Even if you were to fall now, your "friend" would catch you.

Wouldn't it be great to have a friend for every tight spot we find ourselves in? Of course we do: Jesus makes a better anchor than any camming device. Let's trust our safety to our Friend and breathe a sigh of relief. He'll never let us fall.

*It is well for us that as sin lives,
and the flesh lives, and the devil lives,
so Jesus lives; and it is also well that
whatever might these may have to
ruin us, Jesus has still greater
power to save us.*

CHARLES SPURGEON
All of Grace

Lord, the things of this world—including me—all fail.
My ropes, both literal and figurative, will break. Left to
myself, I'll find myself in dangerous spots time and time
again. But You, Father, sent Your Son to save me.
May I trust only in You to catch me when I fall.

Immediately Jesus made his disciples get into the
boat and go on ahead of him to Bethsaida, while
he dismissed the crowd. After leaving them,
he went up on a mountainside to pray.

MARK 6:45–46

Seeing Stars

He alone stretches out the heavens and treads on the waves of the sea. He is the Maker of the Bear and Orion, the Pleiades and the constellations of the south. He performs wonders that cannot be fathomed, miracles that cannot be counted.

Job 9:8–10

In the Dark of Night

Those of us who live in cities—even in much smaller towns—often miss one of the greatest testimonies of God's creative power. That's because "light pollution" can obscure the breathtaking view of the countless stars He hung in the heavens.

But out in the country, far from streetlights, illuminated billboards, and twenty-four-hour gas stations, those stars have a chance to speak a great truth to our souls—a truth that the ancient Job readily understood: God made all of them and the vast sky in which they reside.

When you get the chance to enjoy a truly dark night, take advantage of it. Let the Bear, Orion, the Pleiades—and the thousands of other stars visible to the naked eye—point you to the One who alone stretched out the heavens.

Become lost in God's grandeur.
There can be nothing better,
more productive,
or more rewarding in your life
than to become lost in
great thoughts about a great God.

CHARLES STANLEY
How to Listen to God

Creator God, Your universe is amazing.
The sun, the moon, the stars, the clouds...
and the earth I stand on. Wow! I thank You
that I'm a part of it all—and that I can see
You in it. Remind me, every day, of Your presence
in my life by the creation that surrounds me.

Praise the LORD. Praise the LORD from the heavens, praise him in the heights above. Praise him, all his angels, praise him, all his heavenly hosts. Praise him, sun and moon, praise him, all you shining stars.

PSALM 148:1–3

Song of the Stars

When is the last time you stood alone in the night, watching the stars?

God's handiwork can be millions of miles away—yet as close as a quiet moment in the backyard. Did you ever stop to think that you are seeing the same stars that shone on King David, Christopher Columbus, and George Washington? Those stars were placed on the day God created the heavens—and still point us to our powerful Lord today.

So many of us are caught up in the rat race, searching for peace but missing some of the quiet signposts to God's presence. The night sky holds a million secrets—and waits for us to step away from this hectic world and reach for His hand.

If your life seems to be careening out of control, stop the treadmill. Pull the power cord of your existence for a while, and listen to the song of the stars. Your Creator waits on you, tonight.

God often speaks quietly,
which suggests we need to be
very still in order to hear Him.

BOB BUFORD
Game Plan

Gracious God, my Creator, please help me to
stop racing long enough to hear Your voice—
when I gaze in wonder at the stars.